Ghosts
of North Devon

Peter Underwood

President of The Ghost Club Society

Bossiney Books · Launceston

This book is for
Marilyn and Trevor Kenward
in gratitude

Some other books by Peter Underwood
published by Bossiney Books
Ghostly Encounters
Ghosts of Cornwall
Ghosts of Devon
Ghosts of Dorset
Ghosts of Somerset
West Country Hauntings

This second edition published 2009 by Bossiney Books Ltd
Langore, Launceston, Cornwall PL15 8LD
www.bossineybooks.com
First published 1999
© 1999 Peter Underwood   All rights reserved
ISBN 978-1-906474-13-3
Photographs by Paul White
Printed in Great Britain by R Booth Ltd, Penryn, Cornwall

About the Author

Peter Underwood FRSA is Life President of that famous investigating organisation, The Ghost Club Society, and he must have heard more first-hand ghost stories than any other person alive.

A long-standing member of The Society for Psychical Research, Vice-President of the Unitarian Society for Psychical Studies, a member of The Folklore Society, The Dracula Society and a former member of the Research Committee of the Psychic Research Organisation, he has lectured, written and broadcast extensively.

He took part in the first official investigation into a haunting, and has sat with physical and mental mediums, and conducted investigations at seances. He has also been present at exorcisms and experiments with dowsing, precognition, clairvoyance, hypnotism, and regression. He has conducted world-wide tests in telepathy and extra-sensory perception, and has personally investigated scores of haunted houses.

He possesses comprehensive files of alleged hauntings in every county of the British Isles as well as in many foreign countries, and his knowledge and experience have resulted in his being interviewed and consulted on psychic and occult matters by such organisations as the BBC and ITV.

Born at Letchworth Garden City in Hertfordshire, he now lives in a small village on the Sussex/Surrey border. He is a former Honorary Librarian of The Savage Club, 1 Whitehall Place, London SW1A 2HD, where he can be contacted.

Introduction

Here and there in north Devon you feel, with WG Hoskins, 'impalpable impressions in the air – a sense of something moving to and fro'. There is no denying it. Devon is a haunted county and perhaps especially north Devon which has a magic all its own.

Leafy lanes that meander along in pleasant uncertainty... cream-walled thatched cottages... quaint, sleepy little villages almost slipping into the sea... and the occasional unpretentious town, seething with its special activities – that is north Devon: secret byways, charming coastal towns, famous beauty spots – and ghosts wherever you look!

Alasdair Alpin MacGregor, regarded as something of an authority on ghosts, talked with me at home and in London on many occasions about ghostly activity. Once, I remember, as we were almost deafened by chiming church bells, he told me about the Pine-Coffin family who owned Portledge House in north Devon.

One midnight, many years ago, when the house was tenanted by a family named Crosse, they were all rudely awakened by the tolling of the bells of the nearby church. When the Crosses mentioned the matter to the villagers the next day, they were told that no one else had heard the bells and tolling was not the result of any human hand. Furthermore, the tolling of the bells heard by the occupants of Portledge House was always regarded as a precursor of bad news for the owners. Shortly afterwards the Crosses learned that Mrs Kitson, the Pine-Coffins' daughter, had died suddenly at midnight on the precise date they had heard the bells.

Alasdair Alpin MacGregor was also firmly convinced of the truth of a remarkable story he heard from JW Herries of *The Scotsman*, who devoted a lot of his time to psychical research. He was satisfied the story was factual.

During a country house party at a mansion in north Devon a young woman (who was known to Herries) was a guest. While alone in a room where the table was spread with refreshments, she saw a young man enter by a door on her left. Alasdair later related the story:

'The young man walked across the room. In doing so, he looked hard at her, while she likewise looked at him. He left the room by a door on her right. His appearance so interested her that she asked her hostess about him. Despite her description, and her insistence that she had seen such a person, her hostess was quite unable to identify him. Yet the young woman was positive she had seen someone enter and leave the room in the manner related. Who the unbidden guest could have been, no one had the slightest notion. When in London two years later, the young woman met this elusive, young man. "But I met you before, at such-and-such a house in Devon!" she said, as they were being introduced to one another.

'The young man was surprised at this, declaring that he had never heard of the house, and that he had certainly never been there. The young woman, however, remained convinced of having seen him. "I certainly saw you there!" she insisted. All this, as it happened, provided grounds for friendship. The two of them saw quite a lot of one another thereafter. Eventually they were married.

'Shortly afterwards, the young wife was invited to bring her husband with her to the Devonshire house on a short visit. The evening they arrived there, she took him down to the room where she insisted she had first seen him. "This is where I saw you," she said. "I was standing here. You came in at that door, and went out by the other."

'The husband, looking round the room in some amazement, assured her that he had never been there before. This was the first time that he had ever been in the house, the first time he had ever entered that particular room. In so saying, he passed across the room to make his exit by the second door, *never to be seen again.*

'Herries says that the man disappeared absolutely from all knowledge. The BBC relayed a description of him, and sought information as to his whereabouts, but without avail. From that day to this, nothing has been heard of him.'

(*The Ghost Book*, Robert Hale, 1955, p. 249)

Sadly, typically of such stories, it is impossible to authenticate this remarkable case. Herries was Chairman of the defunct Society for the Recording of Abnormal Happenings in Edinburgh, and I was in correspondence with him back in the 1950s. But Herries is dead now and he was the key to the mystery. It is possible that some of the facts are inaccurate and confused, and that there is a simple explanation – but I suspect we will never know for sure.

North Devon resident, the Viscount of Falkland, late of the 8th Hussars, has told of meeting an elderly couple who had just returned from a motoring holiday in Devon. He was a young man at the time and they told him something he has never forgotten.

They had made an overnight stop at an old house just north of the A30 above Dartmoor which took guests. They arrived a little earlier than the time they had given when booking the room on the telephone, and they spent an anxious few moments ringing the ancient bell at the side of the front door.

Eventually a boy of perhaps thirteen opened the door to them. He seemed rather untidy, very poorly dressed and thoroughly dishevelled, and he said nothing whatsoever to them but picked up their luggage, let them in and disappeared.

They remained in the hall, alone and a little bewildered, for some moments before the wife of the owner arrived and, after apologising for not being there to greet them, she enquired as to how they had managed to get in. When they told her and described the boy, she looked rather startled and, when pressed, said the boy was the house ghost. She said she understood he had once been the bell ringer and door boy when the house had been a monastery, and had died after a severe beating by a monk for some misbehaviour in the 16th century. They were told the ghost house boy did appear from time to time, usually in daylight, and frequently in the vicinity of the ancient front door.

I have tried to make this book as complete as possible, with ghost activity of many kinds and most, if not all, of the reliably reported ghosts in north Devon and some of the colourful legends. The vast majority of the accounts presented here appear for the first time, and I am grateful to all those who have allowed me to publish their experiences.

The Thatched Inn at Abbotsham

For the purposes of this book, I am defining 'North Devon' rather broadly, as everywhere which lies on or north of the A30, excluding Exeter.

My wife and I look back with great pleasure on the time we have spent in north Devon and not least our visits to the pubs, the open spaces, the castles and the great houses in search of their wonderful ghosts. I hope you will let me know if you come across any of them too.

Peter Underwood FRSA
c/o The Savage Club
1 Whitehall Place
London
SW1A 2HD

Abbotsham

Two miles south of Westward Ho!, with its unrivalled cliff walks, stands the old Thatched Inn, once called the New Inn. It is associated with the ghost of a taxi driver who is believed to have carried on an illicit affair with someone at the hostelry many years ago.

The outcome was strange and unexplained: one night, when he was at the wheel of his taxi, it went over a nearby cliff. There were suspicious circumstances, but no one was ever charged with anything and perhaps, as sometimes happens, justice was served in some way we do not understand. The ghostly goings-on of the dead taxi driver are mundane and hardly frightening, consisting of such happenings as clinking glasses, unexplained footsteps and the occasional mysterious movement of objects.

The taxi driver and his paramour were partial to the odd drink, especially advocaat, which used to be served to them in an upstairs room. Doubtless there was much clinking of glasses between them and hurried, furtive footsteps on the stairs and in the corridors.

On occasions to this day, I am told, resident dogs appear to be aware of unseen presences. Once, when a customer asked for a glass of advocaat to be left in the 'haunted' room upstairs – on the taxi driver's birthday as it happened – next morning the glass was found to be empty. I suspect this may not have been due to paranormal activity!

Barnstaple

In August 1998 I was informed by an archivist at North Devon Library and Record Office that one of their office cleaners had spoken of a number of strange phenomena in the former Library, now a museum.

The reported disturbances included unexplained noises of various kinds, movement of objects that were puzzling and inexplicable, and other activity that had no rational explanation. There were also sightings – by different people on different occasions – of a ghostly woman descending a staircase and then walking through a wall at the foot of the stairs.

Several people who worked in the Victorian building claimed to experience a variety of mysterious happenings over a period of months in 1998. Office cleaners, employed by an outside agency and unaware of the apparently paranormal incidents, reported similar disturbances which they were totally unable to explain.

At the time Mrs Maxine Todd, one of the cleaners concerned, told me she and her fellow workers, Brian and Dot, had had so many disturbing and upsetting experiences that she no longer wanted to work there.

During one week she and her companions 'had many things happening... I do wish someone would help put a stop to these odd happenings' she told me. I am seeing what I can do to help.

Barnstaple (Fremington)

Three miles west from Barnstaple, Brynsworthy House at Fremington has long been reputed to be haunted by the ghost of a former Squire Brynsworthy.

According to responsible reports, quoted in the *Transactions of the Devonshire Association*, the ghostly squire used to be seen in the drive leading to the impressive house, mounted on a spectral white horse and holding a glass of wine in his hand.

The shadowy figure was always seen travelling towards the house and the phantom horses' hooves never made a sound on the stony drive, nor did the ghostly rider ever drink the wine.

Among the stories associated with the arresting sight is one where the squire had been in the drawing room at the great house and about to toast his daughter's health on her wedding day when she was accidentally killed outright by a piece of falling masonry. The figure of her father, with glass raised, somehow became frozen in time and the spectre returned time and again, and rode up to the house as he had on that fateful day.

There was a disastrous fire here in 1933 and afterwards reports of the phantom squire grew noticeably fewer and fewer. Perhaps the apparition had at last run its course and faded into nothingness as so many apparitions do eventually.

Oddly enough, although the fire practically gutted the great house, the drawing room which had perhaps seen the tragic event that had such lasting psychic consequences, was the only room not damaged.

Barnstaple (Goodleigh)

A few miles from Barnstaple stands Hall Cottage and in the 1920s two sisters lived here for many years. They grew old and eccentric in the lonely surroundings and soon there were stories that the cottage was haunted and that the old women were really witches. Hardly any villager in the small community would go near the cottage after dark. After the sisters died, it stood empty for years.

Then in the 1970s Reg and Jean Monk found the forlorn building and were busy renovating the by then derelict 17th century cottage when they experienced a series of mysterious happenings. They had bought the place with the sole idea of making it habitable and comfortable, and soon became convinced it was 'very extensively haunted' – they believed they had had encounters with several ghosts, but only one was in any way disagreeable. This was a female phantom whose apparent attempt to crush Jean was resisted and overcome by her will-power.

Reg was a practical man, an interior decorator by trade and an atheist, yet he was the first to see a ghost.

He saw the ghost form (he described it as an 'impression') of a woman of indeterminate age holding what appeared to be a glass jar. She seemed to say something like: 'I have got my treasure and you will have yours.' A few days later Reg and Jean were astonished to unearth a solid silver box in the garden of the cottage.

One bright morning Jean was surprised to see a man (he looked like a farmer) walking across the garden. She called out and went to see what was going on. The 'man' had completely vanished and there was no possible explanation. But Beth, their dog, which had been in the garden at the time, seemed to be frozen with fear and was cowering, with its hair on end.

Soon afterwards Mrs Monk's brother, Owen Scoffield, came to stay, and one night he almost bumped into a man on an upstairs landing, carrying an old-fashioned lantern. No sooner was he aware of the distinct, definite and solid-looking figure than it had disappeared. This was too much for Owen, who spent his nights for the rest of his stay in the back of his car in the garden.

During a power cut the Monks took themselves off to bed by candle light and, after they had been in bed an hour or so, Jean saw a light floating about the room. She drew Reg's attention to it and they both saw it settle near the ceiling. There it grew bigger and bigger until finally it disappeared. They judged they had both watched it for about half an hour.

Local milkman Ivor Evans said at the time that he would not visit the cottage after dark. 'I believe the cottage was empty for something like 40 years after the two elderly sisters died there. They probably resent alterations and improvements. There are a lot of people who have had strange experiences there – anyway, I prefer not to step inside and I'd never go near the place after dark...'

Several years later the Monks told my friend Rodney Legg that the strange happenings were still taking place. Jean said: 'You see things you can't possibly explain: people and animals. We hardly take any notice of them now. There is a lady who comes quite regularly, and a horse and a milkmaid. It seems natural to see these things here and we live side by side with them... the cottage had acquired a very bad reputation over the years and local people would never come up here after dark. That's why it was unoccupied for so long, because of its reputation... we don't say the place is haunted, it's just spirits walking about...'

Bideford

There was a poltergeist infestation here in the 1970s, resulting in a property in North Road being abandoned for demolition after being empty for nearly three years. The last tenants were Mr and Mrs McKenzie who moved out following continual movement of furniture and other inexplicable disturbances.

Benson Herbert of the Paraphysical Laboratory informed me of the case, and said he was impressed by the McKenzies and astonished at the violence of the apparent phenomena. Furniture had moved that would require the strength of two men – and in a locked and sealed room. Once having checked, recorded and ringed the furniture, the investigators were locking and sealing the room when they thought they heard movements from inside. They unlocked the door and discovered a very heavy wardrobe had been moved bodily from one side of the room to the other. It took three men more than ten minutes to move it back to its original position.

So many sounds were reported from the empty house that the police were called and, having made enquiries, they told Benson Herbert they really did not know what they would face when they entered the house to carry out the investigation – they half expected to find a body! But in fact they found nothing, and eventually workmen began the demolition.

During the course of their work, the men employed reported a number of curious and apparently quite inexplicable happenings. Benson Herbert asked to be kept informed of any subsequent disturbances, but he never heard any more.

Bradford

Dunsland House at Bradford near Holsworthy must be counted among the great haunted houses of Devon.

For centuries a panelled room was considered, on the seemingly indisputable evidence of varied witnesses, to be haunted. The ghost of an old lady may have been harmless enough, but she was encountered during the hours of daylight as well as during the dark hours of night and usually when least expected.

A little girl once went into the room when she saw the door was ajar and noticed a figure standing by the window. The child assumed it was a servant, although she did not recollect having seen the woman before, and she went towards the figure to ask about her doll she had mislaid. When she was almost within touching distance, perhaps less than a metre, suddenly the figure was no longer there.

Then there was the young visitor who managed to entice his attractive female cousin into the room on the pretence of admiring the view, and who was about to achieve the results of his ruse – or so he thought – when he saw the girl looking wide-eyed over his shoulder. When he turned, he saw the little old lady standing and looking at them. Before he had time to overcome his confusion, the figure had completely disappeared.

And then there was another occasion when a visiting friend from abroad, who had no knowledge of any ghost at Dunsland, slept in the room and awakened in the dead of night to find an old lady standing at the foot of the bed looking at him. He asked what she wanted, in no uncertain terms, and when he received no reply he angrily got out of bed – only to find the room totally deserted, the doors and windows closed as he had left them. There was no sign at all of the old lady.

For years a great four-poster bed stood in the haunted and usually unoccupied room. On many occasions, when no human being was sleeping in it, the bedclothes were disturbed as though the bed had been occupied by a supernatural sleeper. From time immemorial there has been a family tradition or curse that the house should be owned and lived in by a family and when this ceased the house would disappear. No one knows to which generation the ghostly lady belonged, although it was generally accepted she was a former resident of the house. The estate belonged to the Arscotts, who considerably enlarged the property from 1522 to 1634, when it passed to the Bickford family through the marriage of William Bickford to the Arscott heiress. The property was enlarged again in 1659 and yet again in 1693.

In 1817 it passed by marriage to the Cohams and subsequently to the Dickinsons, who sold it before the Second World War. During the war the house fell into a state of disrepair, but it was bought in 1954 by The National Trust. It had just been fully restored and its furnishings completed when a disastrous fire on 18 November 1967 reduced it to ashes. The ruins, which were dangerous, were demolished, and the only reminder of a haunted house, perhaps destroyed by a curse, is a memorial tablet marking the site.

Looking towards Crow Point, at the southern end of Braunton Burrows. The ferry used to run from near the White House, on the far right, across the estuary to Appledore

Braunton Burrows

South of Braunton, across the water from Appledore, a strange apparition known as White Hat used to be seen, usually in the evening and often after night had fallen. Vernon Boyle remembered his father talking about the odd character, Old White Hat, who used to be seen walking along the beach of Northside, seemingly calling for a passage to Appledore. There was a tradition that any boatman who went ashore to pick up White Hat would not get away alive.

The only story associated with this unusual apparition concerns a tragedy. In the middle of the 19th century a honeymoon couple engaged a boatman to row them across to Appledore one evening, but there was an accident – the boat capsized and the bride drowned. Ever since, the white-hatted bridegroom seeks a boat to take him across the water to his beloved.

My old friend Dan Farson, writer, photographer, broadcaster and Life Member of The Ghost Club Society, became interested in the story after he heard of the ghost with a white hat from his father when they lived at The Grey House (where I used to visit Dan). After he sold that atmospheric house on the seashore and moved to Appledore, he found a number of local people who claimed to have seen the apparition. One summer night, Dan told me, a neighbour hurried round to say he had received a telephone call to say White Hat had been seen. Somewhat reluctantly Dan left his peaceful backyard overlooking the water and set out for Braunton Burrows. There, in the gathering darkness, they both thought they caught a glimpse of a shadowy figure wearing a white hat before it disappeared into the gloom. They then found the friend who had telephoned and it turned out he had seen the figure in the same area, apparently walking up and down, gesticulating and calling out – although no words were heard.

The ghost known as White Hat may have been haunting the same area for over a hundred years. Perhaps it has almost run its course, for most of these ghosts that have their origin in tragic events seem eventually to run down, almost like a battery.

Buckland Brewer

The Coach and Horses pub has long been reputed to be haunted. With its hedgehog-thatched roof, the white-painted hostelry's single entrance porch faces the village roadway that was once the main coaching road south from Bideford.

There have been persistent rumours that the heartless Judge Jeffreys himself held court here, and for years interested visitors were escorted up a narrow flight of steps to an apartment known as the 'the hanging room'. Here, it was said, those found guilty in the 'courtroom' below found their wrists seized and a rope slipped over their heads. A trap door beneath their feet suddenly opened and they dropped to their deaths.

Over the years successive landlords, their wives, staff and visitors to the inn have reported hearing footsteps treading the oak beams

The Coach and Horses at Buckland Brewer

above when no human person is up there. In fact there is conflicting evidence as to whether Judge Jeffreys was ever as far west as Buckland Brewer, but that some traumatic and violent happenings occurred here in the past that have left echoes to this day seems indisputable.

Shadowy forms and indistinct figures have also been reported. One previous landlady always asserted she saw two cavaliers in the corner of the room, close to where the fatal trap door used to be – figures that disappeared as she approached them. Historians have pointed out that in the area there were a number of fierce battles and deadly skirmishes between cavaliers and roundheads.

Some years ago two overnight visitors to the Coach and Horses awakened in the night to find that a ghostly roundhead soldier was approaching the bed! When the couple saw a soldier purposefully coming towards them, they were naturally terrified. But suddenly the figure disappeared and the room was empty and very quiet.

17

Other unexplained sightings at the Coach and Horses include an unidentified female figure in a corridor. The same unknown figure has been reported elsewhere in various downstairs rooms and the unknown lady always appears to be wearing black. The Lady in Black, as this apparition has understandably been named, has now been seen at least half a dozen times by a landlord and various visitors and workers.

Challacombe

Pinkery (or Pinkworthy) Pond lies on Challacombe Common at the western corner of Exmoor. It is supposed to be bottomless, like a number of ponds and lakes in the West Country, and I warned some friends about allowing their adventurous children to play unattended thereabouts when they told me they were touring in the area.

When they returned home, they came round for a drink one evening and, knowing my interest in such matters, said they had to tell me about a most curious experience they had had at Pinkery Pond. They said they were rather tired at the time, having driven quite a few miles, stopped here and there to sightsee, shop and picnic. The children had gone off exploring, and the husband and wife were idly viewing the pond and beyond when they became aware of a man staggering round it. He was some way off and, when they realised he was soaking wet and distinctly distressed, they both got up at the same time to offer help – when to their great astonishment there was no sign of the man they had seen! It seemed impossible that he could have passed out of their sight so suddenly and they both looked carefully round the edge of the pond in case he had fallen, but there was no sign of the strange figure. What did I think of that?

I said nothing, but fetched the 1977 *Transactions of the Devonshire Association* and its 'Report of Folklore'. I showed them an account which detailed the fact that in 1906 a farmer who had drowned himself in Pinkery Pond was seen to reappear around it: you could have heard a pin drop!

Clovelly

To the west of Clovelly, halfway to Hartland, Nether Velly Farm has reputedly long been been haunted by a ghostly cavalier.

When I was there in the 1960s the occupant, Mrs Clark, had no doubt about the matter, for she told me she had seen the ghost many times, as had other residents and the occasional visitor.

There were strong feelings on both sides in North Devon during the Civil War, with one family siding with the Commonwealth and their neighbours aligned to the opposite camp. Properties were confiscated and soldiers on both sides hid, were discovered and murdered or escaped to fight another day. It is more than likely that a cavalier was here once in troubled times and some remnant of his happiness or unhappiness remains and is able to manifest its presence occasionally.

Twenty years after I was at Nether Velly Farm, Antony Hippisley Coxe was there, asking about the ghost and whether it frightened Mrs Clark, when it walked through her sewing room at the back of the house. 'Why no – he is a friend', Mrs Clark replied, 'and has been for these sixty years!'

She pointed out to the puzzled researcher a chair that she regularly put ready for him 'in case he wants to sit down – but he never seems to...' A gentle ghost, this would seem to be, that haunts the place it once knew.

Combe Martin

The splendid St Peter's parish church has a history of hauntings. Soon after the end of the First World War, a man was engrossed in his worship when he happened to glance at the exceptionally fine chancel screen which had once been a rood-loft. What had caught his eye was the screen door opening and from it he watched emerge a solemn procession, a vast concourse of people escorting a mitred bishop and including priests and other laity. All were magnificently attired in rich garments and carrying the various wands of office. Silently the ghostly procession moved down the

aisle and disappeared: one moment they were there, the next there was nothing to be seen. Fifty years later a visitor told me she had had an almost identical experience, and she had not heard of the previous event.

The village also boasts a really original ghost: that of a violinist who wanders through the streets, playing a strangely ethereal kind of music and delighting those who hear him before he abruptly disappears, the strains of his music lingering for a while in the air after the figure has completely gone. The man seems to be a 'country fiddler' of the type that was common until about the end of the 19th century. Sometimes only the ghostly music is heard and no figure is seen, but more often the itinerant performer is witnessed for a moment performing his craft before the street is totally deserted and all is silent.

Crediton

Nearby Downes House was built in the late 1690s. In 1794 it was faced with stone that gave the impression the house was Georgian. In 1842 a large portion at the back was pulled down and an extension was added. In 1910 parts of the interior were altered and in 1980 several rooms at the back were demolished.

Throughout all these years and perhaps as a result of all these alterations (structural changes are notorious for initiating or promoting psychic activity), there have been ghosts and ghostly activity at Downes House.

Mrs Rosemary Parker, the oldest of four girls, was brought up at Downes. She has written of having her own bedroom when she was seven and having a pet Pekinese dog which slept in her bedroom in an old high-backed chair at the end of her bed. The first realisation that there might be something of a ghostly nature in her bedroom came when the dog often used to wake up in the middle of the night, and she began to get the feeling there was someone in the room.

Opposite: St Peter's church, Combe Martin

On one occasion she woke up in the half light of dawn to see a hand stretching towards the little dog which snapped and snarled until it disappeared. The young Rosemary was understandably terrified and tearfully told her parents, but her mother insisted she must have had a bad dream and made her promise not to tell anyone else. After that, Rosemary's pet slept downstairs and she was allowed to leave her bedroom door open with the light on in the passage outside.

Not very long afterwards, Rosemary found herself awake in the middle of the night and she heard voices. She thought they must be coming from one of the bedrooms occupied by her sisters, and she woke the nursery maid. She accompanied the maid to the room from which the voices had appeared to originate, and the nursery maid was more than a little annoyed, for the occupants of the room were all fast asleep.

On the way back to her own room Rosemary heard distinct footsteps shuffling slowly across the stone-flagged passage on the floor below them, but the maid insisted she could hear nothing. Peering down, Rosemary was convinced she could see the stair banisters shaking as whatever was responsible for the footsteps continued up to the stairway and began to mount the stairs. But she was told off in no uncertain terms by the maid who seemed to be utterly convinced the child was making up the whole story.

About an hour later, back in bed in her own room and trying to get to sleep, Rosemary heard the footsteps again. Now they seemed to be returning up the stairs and stopping outside her bedroom door – yet she couldn't see anyone in her dressing-room mirror that reflected the landing outside her room through the ever open door. She was too terrified to move, but eventually everything seemed to return to normal and she went to sleep. Again, when she told her mother, she was assured she had had a dream but, to humour her, she was given a bedroom adjoining her mother's.

One night, in her new bedroom, she awoke to hear the heavy door between the front landing (where her room was situated) and the east wing of the house swinging on its hinges. As she listened, she heard footsteps again, coming along the landing towards the room she was in – and then the bedroom door handle turned quietly. This happened several times and Rosemary called out to her mother in the next room, who told her to fetch her father who was sleeping in the room on the other side of Rosemary's. But Rosemary was too frightened to go alone out on to the landing, so eventually her mother came and fetched her, and together they went to her father's room and woke him.

He comforted Rosemary and, when her parents thought she was asleep, she heard her father whisper to her mother, 'I always knew there was one on the other landing, but I never knew it came on to this one.' It was the first time Rosemary heard someone acknowledge the house had a ghost – or two.

Later, during the Second World War, Downes House was host to a retired naval commander who acted as look-out for German aeroplanes. On several occasions he and others in the house, who had no knowledge of anything untoward ever having been experienced there, complained of hearing odd voices whispering to one another and footsteps during the night which they could not account for. To placate the visitors, the local vicar was asked to carry out a service of exorcism.

That night, according to the family governess, all hell broke loose: there were strange, eerie, loud noises, odd-sounding footsteps, some stealthy and shuffling, and some heavy and determined, and there were strange flashes of light and draughts of icy cold air. Nevertheless for a while after the exorcism things were quiet at Downes House.

Then, in 1947, Rosemary heard footsteps once more. That year there was a large house party and one of the guests telephoned to say he had been delayed by thick fog and would not be able to get to Downes until the early hours of the following day at the earliest. The younger guests and family members, including Rosemary, thought they would have some fun. They tied a torch to the front door handle and made a trail with binder twine from the torch to the delayed guest's bedroom at the far end of the house. They took the trail across the hall by winding it around door knobs, then up the stairs and through a long passage, crossing the twine over one door knob to the opposite one and back to the other side, and so on. There would be great amusement for everyone when the guest arrived, they thought. But it turned out otherwise.

Later that night in bed, Rosemary heard footsteps running straight down the passage, as she had heard so often before, but now there was twine criss-crossed all over the place. No human person could have run along the passage in the state it was in. In the morning the twine was untouched and had to be unravelled before the delayed guest arrived, much later than expected and untroubled by any practical joke.

After Rosemary married, she took over Downes House for a while and during that time the place became very haunted. Her young daughter often woke at the dead of night with the feeling that something was in her bedroom, and her pet cat, which regularly slept on her bed, would also be aware of 'something' and would dive under the bed to escape. Some nights the child heard voices, too, one high-pitched and feminine, the other low and masculine. Some years later, at around midnight, she thought she heard her brother returning from a dance to the room next to hers. She distinctly heard someone get into bed; yet at about 4 o'clock in the morning she was again awakened, this time by the sound of the burglar alarm which her brother had omitted to turn off when he came into the house. Other than one guest who returned with him from the dance, no one else was staying at Downes at the time.

In 1980 parish centenary celebrations were held at Downes House and two marquees were erected on the lawn. Over 600 people attended, including six bishops of various denominations. Next morning at breakfast Rosemary's daughter told her she had found the previous night so noisy she thought that burglars must have been removing all the furniture. She had become so frightened she didn't dare leave her bedroom.

After that night, Rosemary Parker heard the Downes ghost on only one occasion. She decided the presence of all those bishops frightened it! I wonder.

Crediton (Coleford)

Four miles west of Crediton you will find this village and its thatch-roofed inn that dates back to the 13th century. Not that eight centuries count when it comes to naming such a delightful hostelry – it's called The New Inn, would you believe.

Here the ghost of a monk is known by the name of Sebastian, and he is thought to have been murdered long ago when he came upon a gang of rustlers sharing out their ill-gotten gains. When he refused to turn a blind eye to what he had seen, they silenced him once and for all. Little did they expect his ghost would return to the scene of his sudden and violent demise at the hands of rogues who were caught and punished within days. But for the murder of Sebastian, they would never have been suspected. Perhaps that is why Sebastian still roams this ancient inn, reminding us all that violation of the law can have curious repercussions.

In 1998 a barmaid at The New Inn said Sebastian was still very much around. In fact, he had thrown a bucket at her in the cellar within the past two weeks and a glass had mysteriously tumbled down while she was alone at the bar. Brother Sebastian, it seems, has much to answer for!

Left: The King's Head, Cullompton, haunted by the ghost of an American airman

Opposite: The Manor Hotel

Cullompton

Many of the picturesque and haunted pubs in Devon have phantoms from another age: cavaliers, roundheads, monks and nuns, figures in attire from history, and the occasional ghost animal. Here at The King's Head at Cullompton the ghost is of more recent days, the result, it seems, of an argument during the Second World War.

There was a period when American servicemen in Britain, and particularly airmen, were unpopular for one reason or another. The British had survived all Hitler could throw at them and they knew they owed a tremendous debt of gratitude to the men of the Royal Air force who fought courageously, often against great odds. Then the Americans came, with much talk of their own achievements and the British airmen were away on duty. At times tempers flared, especially when oiled with beer or local cider.

During one such confrontation in the public bar of The King's Head, an American airman received a stab wound that killed him. Such a shocking event seems to have left behind echoes of that fateful fight and occasionally, especially when a feeling of suspense or shock or horror fills the air, the phantom form of a young man in the uniform of the American Air Force is glimpsed for a brief moment at the spot where his life came to a sudden and violent end.

Nearby the Manor Hotel has a haunted room where a young lady was jilted on her wedding day. Room 6 may have been where she breathed her last in some forgotten tragedy, but whether this sad event happened when the property was a hotel or whether it was earlier when it was a private house has never been established. At all events the tragic happening seems to have left behind a visual reminder that, some say, occasionally manifests to those who dare to occupy the haunted room.

Yet another Cullompton hostelry guards its secrets just as jealously. The White Hart has a hidden room with no door – what its purpose is or was no one seems to know. Much the same applies to room 8 where the ghost is known as Angie. Her presence and the sound of children playing in the room and on the landing outside have been reported from time to time, and usually in the small hours of the morning.

What event or series of events, I wonder, triggered and established such a haunting whose remnants linger on, mystifying and intriguing those fortunate enough or unfortunate enough to encounter Angie and her brood of ghostly children?

Great Torrington

A Battle of Torrington was fought here in 1646 and a soldier who died in that conflict still haunts the castle hill. In 1995 three visitors were astonished to see a war-worn man in tattered period uniform staggering down Castle Hill. They thought at first it must be someone taking part in a local event until they noticed blood pouring down the man's face from a gaping wound in his head. As they went to help, he disappeared in front of their eyes and they discovered that no one else had seen anything. A case perhaps of being in exactly the right place at exactly the right time.

Here we are also in the heart of North Devon Black Dog country and there are many reports of such creatures or semi-creatures or psychic creatures being seen. A few years ago former Bideford mayor, Frank Bailey, and three friends, including Dr Simon Trezise, were astounded when 'a large black dog suddenly appeared in their headlights, coming towards them. Dr Trezise jammed the brakes on to avoid it and the dog veered off and disappeared as suddenly as it had appeared.'

Antony Coxe told me he spoke to two people in 1972 who had encountered a black dog or black hound on the Torrington to Bideford road. This is very much a part of the haunt of the Black Hound and evidence is quite overwhelming that some 'animals' which have been seen here are not of this world.

Great Torrington (Roborough)

About five miles east of Great Torrington in a delightful mid-Devon valley a farmer and his wife were driving towards Roborough one day when they saw a funeral cortege approaching. The farmer drew his trap into the side of the lane and waited for the funeral to pass. It seemed to take some time for the whole procession slowly to go by, but eventually the last man passed. Giving him a moment to walk out of earshot, the farmer looked round to ensure that it was clear for him to pull out into the lane. To his enormous astonishment, the whole cortege had disappeared. As far as he could see, the road was completely deserted, and he and his wife looked at

Great Torrington, the castle hill

each other unbelievingly. It was something they remembered to their dying days.

All this happened a very long time ago (the story is included by a student of folklore in his collection published in 1976) and would hardly have been worth including here had it not been that in 1997 a correspondent wrote to me after he'd read a profile of me in one of the national dailies. He mentioned an odd experience that happened to him and his wife in the summer of 1997 in mid-Devon.

In a lane just outside Roborough (as my correspondent later established) he and his wife had enjoyed a roadside picnic and were about to continue on their way when they saw a funeral procession approaching. They waited for it to pass – it was going in the same direction as themselves, towards Roborough.

They were more than a little surprised at the size and nature of the cortege: the hearse was drawn by black horses with black plumes on their heads, and the undertakers, walking beside the hearse and horses, wore long black mourning suits and top hats.

The rest of the long line of mourners all seemed to be dressed in old-fashioned clothes and walked with their heads down. There was a strange quiet while the procession passed, broken only by the slight jingle of the harnesses and the sound of feet on the roadway. At last it had completely passed, and my correspondent and his wife looked at each other, realising the funeral would hold them up. However, they decided to set off anyway – perhaps it would turn off and allow them to get to Roborough and beyond.

Imagine their surprise when they discovered the road ahead absolutely clear. There were no turnings the procession could have taken, and they sped into Roborough in minutes. The next day they mentioned to a local man what they had seen, but he pretended not to hear and went on his way. A local shopkeeper totally ignored what they said when they began to describe their experience, and they soon gave up and never did find a solution to the curious incident. They had never heard of such a thing happening in the vicinity of Roborough or anywhere else.

Hartland

Three miles south of Hartland on the A39 stands, as it has done for over 300 years, a former coaching inn. Spring and autumn fairs were sometimes held at the back of the remote inn and whatever the weather the scene was a colourful one: farmers, smallholders, local people, visitors and travelling people all turned up in various costumes hoping to do deals of one sort or another.

The story goes that a handsome young gypsy lured an attractive seventeen-year-old away from her family and for a while they lived together happily enough. But then things went wrong, and one night during an angry quarrel the gypsy knocked the girl to the ground and she died.

It is her ghost that is reputed to haunt the inn to this day. Local author Antony Hippisley Coxe told me that her quick running footsteps have been heard on numerous occasions – indeed he had heard them himself and was satisfied that no mortal being was responsible. Dogs (good psychic barometers, Elliott O'Donnell used to say) have repeatedly become suddenly frightened just before the mysterious footsteps begin. Their fear and distress are evident from the way they cower on the floor, eyes fixed on something invisible to their human companions and with their fur standing on end along their backs.

From time to time visitors with no knowledge of the story of any haunting ask about the 'presence' they have been aware of and how it was that the bedroom curtains they had drawn before going to bed were pulled back in the morning.

According to one author and researcher, for a few years 'many' people claimed to see the figure of a young girl, but sightings have been few and far between during the last twenty years or so. One former landlord, Alan Higgins, however, used to say that he and his family heard the running footsteps on scores of occasions and once, hearing them run upstairs, he immediately thought of an intruder whom he decided to catch in the act. There are two staircases to the upper storey of the inn. Grabbing a rolling pin for protection, the landlord bounded up one staircase, leaving his wife to guard the other. An immediate and thorough search revealed no human intruder and nothing to account for the footsteps which had been heard by all the family.

The immediate vicinity of the parish church at Hartland, dedicated to St Nectan, is haunted by a ghostly procession of monks (the haunted road runs beside Hartland Abbey) and the Rev. Harold Lockyer saw a ghost monk inside the church. Evidence suggests there are more ghostly monks and nuns than any other recognised ghost. While some people may say surely nuns and monks should rest in peace if any of us should, I have long been convinced that concentrated thought has a lot to do with ghostly activity. That puts a new complexion on the whole case for haunting nuns and monks and haunted churches, rectories and vicarages.

There have been stories and reports for centuries of two ghostly ladies being seen near Bow Bridge at Hartland. They appear to wear beautiful silken dresses which can be heard to rustle as they move: indeed they might be taken for two ladies in period costume dress walking home were it not for the fact that both figures

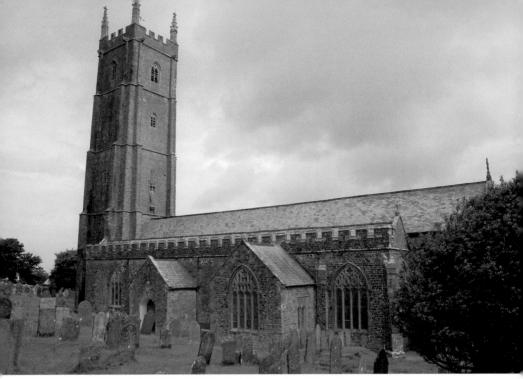

St Nectan's at Stoke, the parish church of Hartland

are headless. The Devonshire Association included details of the arresting sight in their 34th Report.

The same report contains an account of strange spectral lights in the same area. On one occasion distinct globes of light were seen which were about 18 inches (45 cm) in diameter. Another witness told me the lights seemed to bounce on the ground up to a height of 20 or 30 feet (6 or 9 metres). All those who have seen the lights say they are really beautiful, not at all glaring, and almost ultramarine in colour at the base. They are usually seen for about a minute before completely and suddenly disappearing – until the next time.

Animal ghosts seem to abound in Hartland, with a snow-white horse walking steadily along Blind Road (a private road through Hartland Abbey Park to Blackpool Hill) and the ghost of a calf appearing on Docton Bridge on certain nights. For years people avoided the bridge after dark for fear of encountering a ghost animal. Why it should appear is a mystery yet to be solved.

Hatherleigh

Hatherleigh, north of Okehampton, is an attractive little town with a comfortable and popular thatch-roofed hotel, The George, dating back to the 14th century.

Once a favourite stopping place for horse-drawn carriages linking north and south Devon, it is appropriate that a phantom coach and horses has been heard to clatter up to The George, especially on wet winter evenings. There are local people and visitors today who claim to have seen this striking spectacle and many more who insist without the shadow of a doubt that they have heard the clip clop of horses' hooves and the sound of wheels and straining leather where there has been no sign of anything to account for such noises. Indeed I have to say that on one occasion my wife and I heard the unmistakable sounds of a horse-drawn vehicle pulling up outside the inn, followed by complete silence. We discovered nothing whatever that could possibly have accounted for what we experienced.

Inside the hostelry there are other ghosts that might be encountered on summer nights as well as winter ones. Among the odd and

unexplained happenings inside The George have been the sudden rush of cold air that has no logical explanation; the appearance of a transparent woman – an odd and frightening apparition that drifts along a corridor and disappears; and the occasional sound of voices from areas devoid of human beings.

No clear words have ever been distinguished in the low muttering sounds that have been heard in different parts of this haunted inn. There have also been reports of a naked female phantom: one of several in my records.

One couple staying at the inn had retired for the night when they both experienced a sudden gust of cold air that chilled the room. When the husband left the room to see what could be done, he saw the spectre of a woman gliding noiselessly along the corridor outside. She seemed to be surrounded by an aura of supernatural glowing light, through which the familiar details of the corridor and its furnishings could just be made out.

Perhaps the phantom lady is looking for someone; perhaps she walks in remorse for something she has done; perhaps she walks again as she did for the last time in life along that corridor. The fact is no one knows who she was or why she walks, but that she occasionally does so accompanied by a chill draught of icy air is certain – if human testimony is to be relied upon.

Heddon's Mouth

The area around Heddon's Mouth, between Lynton and Ilfracombe, is associated with paranormal occurrences. This spot, in common with many parts of the area, was once the domain of smugglers, and there have been many people who claim to have caught a glimpse of misty figures lurking hereabouts, looking down at the angry waters, especially on stormy nights. The sounds of oaths, straining men and horses, shouts and the occasional dull thud have all been reported.

Not very long before his death, my friend Antony Hippisley Coxe (especially known for his excellent *Haunted Britain*, 1973) told me he and a fellow-writer named Kendall Lane were working on a

Looking down on Heddon's Mouth from the coast path

series of programme proposals for a television series, and they took a walk together.

Antony had completed a book, *Smuggling in the West Country between 1700 and 1850*. He took Kendall Lane down to Heddon's Mouth where he recalled the story he had unearthed of a smuggling lugger that came in too close to the shore to avoid capture and was wrecked, losing all hands. As he described how 'batmen' protected the 'tubmen' who brought 'half-ankers' of brandy up the cliff to load on to ponies, sometimes shaven and covered with cart grease to get the contraband inland as quickly as possible, he noticed his friend had been recording it all.

When the tape was played back, there appeared to be a distinct clip clop of hoof beats! Kendall Lane had the tape 'blown up' so that the sounds could be analysed and the answer was: horses' hooves. Certainly there were no horses, ponies or donkeys anywhere around Heddon's Mouth at the time.

Ilfracombe

One of Devon's leading resorts, with its historic natural harbour set amidst spectacular scenery and dominated by Lantern Hill, Ilfracombe should not be missed – I have lost count of the number of times my wife and I have visited Ilfracombe and climbed Lantern Hill, although we have not seen a ghost. Joan Dimond was luckier.

Joan Dimond tells me she is a medium, and seeing and hearing things that are not visible or audible to others has long been part of her life. The ghost she met at Ilfracombe is typical of many such encounters she has experienced. He told her his name was David and that he had been a draper's assistant in the town before he contracted typhoid and succumbed at the age of twenty-three. Here is the story of Joan's meeting with David in her own words:

'During the latter part of March 1998 I had reason to visit Ilfracombe. It was a cool day, clear but not much in the way of sunshine. I decided to buy fish and chips for lunch before leaving for home. My car was parked in the Pier Car Park below Lantern Hill.

'Lantern Hill is quite a landmark. A high rugged outcrop jutting into the sea is crowned by a small stone-built chapel. The chapel is reached via a winding path. Lantern Hill provides an excellent lookout post across the Bristol Channel. Also, as far as I was concerned, an excellent place to choose to eat my fish and chips. Particularly as I had never been up Lantern Hill before.

'I set off up the winding path, the cliff face on one side and the sea crashing on the rocks below me on the other. As I approached a steep flight of steps near the summit I paused, debating whether to go to the very top or not. I don't like heights. There was a hand rail though, and it didn't look too bad. I reached the bottom of the steps and looked up.

'Near the top of the steps, looking down at me and smiling, stood a young man. He came down the steps towards me. He was dressed in a black frock coat and a stove pipe hat. He wore slim trousers.

Opposite: Ilfracombe Harbour, with the Lundy ferry at her mooring. The little hill behind her is called Lantern Hill, because the Chapel of St Nicholas on its summit was once used as a lighthouse

I gained the impression they were dark grey or black. He was not very clear from the knees down, so it is difficult to say. He was not solid in appearance. I could still see the steps behind him. He had fair side whiskers very neatly trimmed. In height I would guess him to be about 5 feet 10 inches [1.78 m] and he was of slim build. In short a smart young man of perhaps 24 or so who looked very pleased to see me.

'He held out his right hand to me as he came to the bottom of the steps, obviously intent on making sure I got up the steps safely. I set off up to meet him. His hand did not feel cold or solid. Instead the feeling I had when he reached out for my hand was one of warmth and friendship. I could feel the pressure of his hand under mine as I was gently led up the steps. He walked in front travelling up sideways and still looking down at me and positively beaming with pleasure. The feeling was mutual. He vanished from my sight at the top of the steps, but I was fully aware he was still with me. I could sense where he was all the time. I ate my fish and chips, admired the view and then set off back to the car park. He remained with me all the way back to the car.'

An old travel guide to north Devon describing Ilfracombe and its curiosities refers to the ghostly 'vicarage children' who had been murdered for their inheritance. They haunted their room which was situated over the kitchen, sighing and sobbing. They were apparently heard and seen by many people: 'two beautiful children richly dressed standing in the sunlight', but sadly the exact location of the haunted property is not given.

Long ago a Jewish pedlar was murdered at Cairn Top and his ghost reputedly haunts the bushes thereabouts. There are many reports which suggest the area is haunted, and probably just as many experiences are not reported.

While staying at Ilfracombe some years ago, my wife and I wandered up Cairn Top one lovely sunny day, and were surprised in the balmy mid-afternoon to catch a glimpse of a stooping and untidy middle-aged man carrying a battered suitcase in one hand and with what looked like half a dozen small saucepans strung together in the other. He disappeared behind a tall bush and my wife, worried he might have slipped and fallen, asked me to make sure he was all right.

Cautiously I approached the bush and walked all round it. There was no sign of the man we had both seen and heard so distinctly. Nor did there appear to be any possible place he could have gone without our seeing him. Back at our hotel we mentioned what had happened and then learned for the first time about the ghost of the murdered Jewish pedlar. Did we catch sight of this phantom pedlar? We have often wondered.

Ilfracombe (Chambercombe Manor)

Nearby Chambercombe Manor is beautifully situated in a secluded valley and may date from the 11th century, although most of the present structure is probably of 16th century origin.

The property is mentioned in Domesday Book and today contains eight rooms of period furniture, a priest hole and a haunted room. It has fascinating historical associations and a ghost story as good as any in the county.

There are records which show the original house as being in the possession of Sir Henry de Champernowne, who was lord of the manor of Ilfracombe in 1162. The manor was in the hands of the Champernownes until the 15th century when the branch of the family became extinct and the property eventually passed to the Duke of Suffolk, father of Lady Jane Grey, who is said to have slept in the room above the hall when on a visit.

In 1686 the days of prosperity ended and the land was split up and sold to various buyers. The manor became a farmhouse, which it remained for many years (and it also became in all probability the haunt and hide-out of smugglers and wreckers). The elegant rooms seen today may well once have been used as cattle sheds, store rooms and farm living rooms. But fortunately the various owners and occupants seem to have respected the ancient structure and they did little harm, so that today it is easy enough to sense the former grandeur of Chambercombe.

In 1865 the then tenant was making some repairs to the outside of the house when he discovered the outline of a window for which

Chambercombe Manor, Ilfracombe

he could find no corresponding room. Breaking through the wall in the interior of the house led to the discovery of a secret chamber wedged between Lady Jane Grey's room and the one that for a long time it was thought adjoined it.

They found a well-furnished apartment, including a handsome four-poster bed still hung with rotting curtains. The tenant fetched a candle and explored the dusty and cobweb-laden apartment – and came across more than he expected when he moved the curtains: on the bed lay the skeleton of a woman, a few fragments of rich tapestry draped here and there, and the skull seemed to grin in the dim candlelight.

The story goes that she was a titled lady from Spain visiting relatives at Chambercombe. When her ship was wrecked near Hele, she was captured by wreckers and conveyed through a secret passage that existed at one time between Chambercombe Manor and the beach. (The entrance to this passage was found in 1900, but the tunnel has long since fallen in.) The girl was robbed of her valuables and walled up in her grave of a room and left to die.

Another story has it that the body was that of Kate Oatway, the daughter of William Oatway, a noted wrecker who lived at Chambercombe in the 17th century. Did he, as has been suggested, kill his own daughter after she had threatened to denounce him to the authorities when he would not agree to her marriage to a rival wrecker's son? It would not have been too difficult to seal the body into what became a secret room.

Whatever the truth of the matter, once the skeleton had been found and buried in a pauper's grave, the Secret Room became the Haunted Room where weird sounds were heard at night. Even to this day such disturbances are reported – the ghost of a distressed young woman has been seen in and around the room where the skeleton was revealed.

Daniel Farson, representing The Ghost Club Society, looked into the mysteries of Chambercombe very thoroughly and was able to report, in print, 'the ghost of Kate Oatway... haunts Chambercombe Manor today. She is seen constantly.' The custodian at the time stated, 'We hear noises, we put a key on a particular hook and it has moved when we come back – and visitors have seen her passing *through* our guide!'

The form of the ghost never varies, it seems. Reports say the figure is 'tall and smiling, dressed in grey'. When the manor was owned by Mr LC Pincombe, a guide was taking some visitors up the Elizabethan staircase when he noticed a young lady join the group. He had not seen her previously and assumed she had arrived late. He noticed her as they explored several rooms, but when they descended into the courtyard she had vanished. He never did find out who she was.

Dan Farson said the figure was reliably seen on two occasions in 1976 and Air Commodore Carter Jonas told me, after visiting the house, that there were reports of the ghost of Kate Oatway having been seen in 1980 and 1989. Richard Hayward told Roy Harley Lewis he had no personal knowledge of any sightings of the ghost, although he was conscious of several 'cold spots' in the house that had been remarked upon by other people. In fact on a number of occasions visitors have been so upset when they have encountered these cold spots and the 'atmosphere' in some parts of Chambercombe Manor that they have left without finishing the tour. The manor is now owned by a charitable trust and is open to the public from Easter until October, but it is advisable to check times of opening.

Ilfracombe (Hele Bay)

The Old Corn Mill and Pottery at Hele Bay is well worth a visit. Bill Briggs was the miller here in 1948 and several of his relatives have visited the mill and vouch for the story that one day a vicious rat seized Bill by the throat and he died as a result. During one restoration of the building (the mill dates from 1525), just one dead rat was found and its shrunken carcass was preserved. Was it the rat that had killed the miller? At all events the previous owners kept the relic and it looks down on visitors to the mill...

Luther Solway was Bill Briggs' father-in-law and he was the miller responsible for the 1927 restoration which he carried out when he inherited the mill from his father. He died slowly and horribly from 'millers' lung' – silicosis caused by inhaling flour dust. People still living in Hele today remember the old mill being so full of dust that it was virtually impossible to see across the room, and the old miller coughing and gasping so badly he could hardly stand up.

Care is taken to avoid mentioning the name of the third miller who met his death here – in case it upsets him, for his ghost still haunts the mill. It is known that he was very strong and used to carry the heavy 200 pound (90 kg) bags of grain on his back up the narrow stairs rather than use the chain hoist. One day his old coat caught in the moving cogs when he was working alone in the evening and he was slowly mangled to death, his screams unheard.

When I visited, the then owners, Robin and Sue Gray, told me that a lot of people visiting the place for the first time sense the presence of ghosts who, the majority claim, are friendly. Others, however, come out of the mill quickly and in fear. But ninety per cent of visitors feel and hear nothing out of the ordinary. One

Hele Mill, near Ilfracombe

group claim to have photographed the ghost and they visit Hele Mill from time to time, sitting quietly in the mill at dusk to see if the ghost puts in an appearance.

A previous owner, Mr Lovell, used to say that at least two visitors ran out of the mill because they felt the presence of a ghost and once Lovell even saw the ghost himself. He was watching the level of the grain slowly sinking down in one of the bins on the top floor as it slid down the chute. Suddenly he was aware of an old man smoking a clay pipe and wearing a dirty and tattered old macintosh standing beside him. Lovell thought the old man spoke, saying 'However many times you watch it, it is always fascinating...'

Lapford

Off the A377 north-west of Crediton you come to Lapford where the ghost of St Thomas à Becket of Canterbury is supposed to gallop through the village at midnight on St John's Eve (27 December) on his way to Nymet Rowland, where one of the knights who murdered Becket is said to have built the church as part of his penance. Or perhaps it should be Nymet Tracey, a home of Sir William de Tracy, who almost certainly did build a church at Bovey Tracey in south Devon in penance?

It might be thought curious that the ghost is said to appear two days before the anniversary of Becket's death, but as Dr Charles Sampson observed more than sixty years ago, 'the periodicity of apparitions can come around with extraordinary accuracy'. Some manifestations do seem to occur regularly, especially on certain holy days such as St Mark's Day (5 March), St Anthony's Day (13 June), All Hallows Eve (31 October) and St John's Eve (27 December). When I compiled a ghost calendar a few years ago, I pointed out that there are many puzzling factors about ghosts which seem to appear on the same date, irrespective of leap years or alterations in the calendar.

The fact remains that there is good evidence for some ghosts appearing only on certain days and there could be an important and crucial cyclic element to these happenings we have yet to discover.

According to Antony Coxe, Lapford has another ghost. In the middle of the 19th century the rector, John Arundel Radford, murdered his curate but was acquitted because his parishioners 'had never hanged a parson yet and weren't going to start now'. The rector terrorised his parishioners with his fierce pack of hounds, fathered innumerable illegitimate children, and outwitted his bishop, according to Theo Brown. One of his servants even drowned herself in the rectory pond when she discovered she was pregnant. Radford lived on for several more years and asked to be buried in the chancel of his church – or he would return to haunt the village. The authorities refused to give the necessary permission, and the murdering rector was buried outside the vestry door in the churchyard. There have been numerous stories of his ghost being seen here.

Luffincott

In this remote parish in the extreme west of the county you will find what is left of the abandoned little church of St James, and the nearby former rectory was a haunted place.

The trouble centred around the Rev. Franke Parker, a bachelor who lived alone in the rectory he had rebuilt, and there are many odd tales told about this strange man who was rector from 1838 until he died in 1883, a period of forty-five years – there is no doubt he came to love the place. He is reported as repeatedly saying that no successor would ever dispossess him of what he had come to regard as his own.

He was something of a fanatical book collector, and almost starved himself and lived an exceptionally frugal existence in order to buy rare old editions (which he bequeathed on his deathbed to Truro Library). He was heard to say time and time again that no one would ever take over his domain and he should be buried deep so that he could not rise again and seek revenge. It has been said he owned some books that he would never allow his servants to see, and he always insisted on all members of his household, no matter how humble, joining him daily in saying matins and at evensong in the church.

He would sit up until all hours, sometimes with local people but more often on his own, and he was known suddenly to stand up and bark like a dog before resuming his seat as though nothing had happened. Small wonder that some folk believed he could turn himself into a dog or a lion. Once a messenger came to a public house to call one of his servants to return to the rectory where Parson Parker was 'ever so queer'. He was sitting up in bed having fixed himself up like a toad and he was croaking...

After Parker's death his two immediate successors left after very short incumbencies – perhaps they sensed the presence of Parson Parker, even if they did not see his ghost. The third incumbent was the Rev. T W Browne, another bachelor, stout, with a pointed beard. Parishioners regarded him as 'a queer old chap', but the interesting thing is that after a while he too refused to live in the rectory and went instead to nearby Clawton.

It seems that one evening while he was enjoying his lone meal at Luffincott Rectory he glanced up from the book he was reading and saw the ghost of Parker, his predecessor, standing and looking at him. Browne walked out of the rectory and hastened to Clawton where he had been curate, and took up his former lodgings there. He never entered Luffincott Rectory again, nor would he allow any of his possessions to be brought out of the house.

As the story spread, parishioners and neighbours would peer into the deserted rectory 'to see if parson's things were still there'. His hats and coats, books and furniture, and just about everything else in the rectory soon disappeared. Before long people, alone, in couples and in parties, spent nights in the deserted and haunted rectory, hoping to see some supernatural visitation. A few years later, either by accident or design, the house caught fire and was burned down.

My friend James Turner, who was fascinated by Luffincott and its incumbents, showed me a letter he had received from the Rev. John Scott (himself rector of Luffincott for eight years) in which he reported evidence from a lady who lived in the parish. One day, soon after Parson Browne had left Luffincott Rectory in such a hurry, he had called to see her. After chatting to her for a while, he turned as white as a sheet and, pointing to a photograph on the mantelpiece, asked who the man was. 'Why,' he was told, 'that's Parson Parker'. And Browne exclaimed, 'That's the man I saw in the rectory that night...'

Luffincott had a haunted atmosphere when I was there twenty years ago; perhaps it still has. And perhaps the ghost still walks, for I have had reports of a figure in clerical garb disappearing in mysterious circumstances in the immediate area of the old rectory.

Lundy Island

In the Bristol Channel twelve miles off Hartland Point sits the wonderful granite island of Lundy with its lighthouses, hotel, remains of Marisco Castle, round towers, pirate gold and a ghost-haunted cave.

Once a stronghold of smugglers and, in the 17th century, a hiding place for pirates and foreign privateers, it is now a haven for birds, especially puffins. There is also a wealth of rare wild flowers to be found on the thousand acres comprising the island, many of them pasture. The landing at the south-east of Lundy Island is sheltered by tiny Rat Island, where the once common black rat still survives. There are some prehistoric remains on Lundy Island and the foundations of an ancient chapel dedicated to St Helen.

For a long time it has been suspected that pirate gold is buried on Lundy – with the sea and two ghosts keeping guard over it. The best known treasure was that collected by Captain Robert Nutt, a bold and bloodthirsty buccaneer who plundered ships belonging to rich British merchants in the 17th century. For three years he used Lundy as his headquarters and then one night as he was returning from a raid in his ship, *Black Mary*, he found himself being chased by two English men-of-war.

He had already hidden his treasure, prepared for just such an eventuality, but now he was forced to flee the island, and in the chase his ship foundered off the Welsh coast with the loss of all hands. The cave harbouring the ghosts and holding the treasure is, by all accounts, on the west side of the island at the bottom of a 365 foot (111 metre) cliff. The entrance to it is on a level with the Atlantic at high tide and within a stone's throw of the wreck of *HMS Montague* that has been there since 1906.

Some years ago an intrepid special correspondent from a national newspaper attempted to locate the treasure. Having acquainted himself with the lay of the land – and the sea – he posted a guard at the mouth of the cave and arranged for him to fire a blank shot as a warning when the tide reached a certain point. This was an essential precaution, for when it is high tide the sea reaches far into the cave. Indeed, only on the calmest of days is anyone able to approach the entrance in any safety.

The explorer now set out to see what he could find inside the ominous-looking cave. After negotiating piles of flotsam and jetsam and wreckage of all kinds that probably went back centuries, he came to a barrier of rock. Flashing his torch through a narrow aperture in the stones and rubble he saw a skull!

The skull partly obscured his view as to what lay beyond and, thrusting his hand into the gap, he succeeded in gently pushing it to one side. He was then able to focus the torch on the ledge of rock on which the skull had lain, and he saw by torchlight the rest of the skeleton – and another one beyond.

This then was the explanation of the strange disappearance of two islanders who, in 1864, set out to recover Nutt's treasure. They had evidently been trapped in the cave by a fall of rock and then the cave had flooded. The resulting barrier effectively barred any entry to the cave – and to the treasure.

Lighting up the cave as best he could by sweeping the light from his torch to and fro through the aperture, he saw a rough circle of piled-up stones in the centre of the chamber. He decided it must be about 3 feet (1 metre) high and 25 feet (8 metres) in circumference, and could only be the work of humans. He was unable to see over the edge, but where a stone had fallen from the top of the pile he seemed to discern a blotch of russet brown, and his heart leapt as he realised it had all the appearance of the rounded lid of a rusty iron chest. As he peered hard at whatever was within the circle of stones, something caught his eye, right at the back of the cave or as far as he could see: something had moved! He directed the beam of his torch as far as he could in the relevant direction, but he could not distinguish anything. Then something moved to his left and he turned the direction of his torch again, as quickly as he could in the limited space he had at his disposal, but could detect nothing to account for what he had seen.

He looked again at his surroundings. Nothing but powerful explosive could move the barrier of rock and such an explosion could well bring tons more rock crashing down, thereby creating an even greater obstruction. Defeated in his search for Nutt's treasure, and more than a little aware of the possibility the cave was indeed haunted, he retreated and wrote up his report.

More recently, my friend Daniel Farson had the same idea, but his enquiries on Lundy revealed that the islanders believe there is a curse on the treasure. They insisted the cave is haunted by two buccaneers whom Nutt murdered there to dissuade treasure seekers and perhaps guard the bounty with their ghosts. The ghosts of the two islanders who had ventured into the cave and never returned are also thought to haunt it. Dan had high hopes of a television film about Nutt's treasure but, although he did make one attempt to get deep into the cave, he gave up after a few hours and never made another. The film was never made. I asked him several times about what he had found, but he always said, 'You really wouldn't want to know', and invariably and hastily changed the subject.

Captain Robert Nutt's treasure is probably still there waiting for someone brave enough to overcome the elements and the ghosts.

Lynton

In September 1998 I heard of a ghost dog that has long been seen and heard in the vicinity of Bridge Ball, Lynton. It is a black labrador-type dog and it seems drawn to a 400-year-old cottage where

Miss Valerie H Goold has seen the apparition several times. She and her father have heard the ghost dog on four occasions.

Once, when Miss Goold and her father were away in Cornwall on a sailing holiday, a friend from the Midlands called unexpectedly. Afterwards he wrote to say how sorry he was to have missed them, but that the dog sounded very ferocious! Asked what he meant by this, since their dog was 120 miles away with them, both the friend and his wife swore they heard a dog barking and snuffling inside the front door when they called.

Miss Goold tells me she has actually felt the 'ghost dog' touch her with its nose on several occasions and she did not find it at all frightening. Several people visiting the cottage have said they feel a very friendly, comfortable feeling when they enter the particular room where the dog has been heard and felt. In October 1998 Miss Goold also told me that other people as well as herself have actually seen the ghost dog, 'one of these sightings in fact being within the last seven days'. An old lady who lived in the village for about fifty years told them that many years ago a dog was drowned in the river which runs through the cottage property.

Martinhoe

In the middle of some of the most beautiful scenery in north Devon, a few miles to the west of Lynton and overlooking National Trust land and delightful Woody Bay, you will find Martinhoe. Here, according to firsthand evidence which I possess, a ghost monk walks.

In 1989 five young people spent a holiday in the Heddon Valley, staying in cabins at Martinhoe Manor. One evening they decided to walk to the Woody Bay Hotel for a drink. David Crawford, who sent me the initial account, emphasised they had consumed *no* alcohol before they reached Woody Bay and before they encountered 'something' they were totally unable to explain. The five included David himself, his sister Lisa, their brother Darran, a friend Lorraine and another friend Terry. Their ages ranged from seventeen to twenty-eight.

The track they followed was rather dark and narrow, being bordered by trees with overhanging foliage, and it became narrower still where there is a steep drop to the left, just past Inkerman Bridge. Here it was so dark and dim that although they could hear the rushing water, they could not see it. Terry was walking ahead at the time, shining his torch to guide the rest of the party who linked arms for safety. The two girls walked together.

Suddenly, and without warning, close to some ancient and worn steps, Lorraine felt a little tug on her cardigan and she asked who was fooling around, but no one admitted to touching her. Then the same thing happened again, and she swung round and demanded to know who was responsible. Before anyone could answer, Lisa turned round too and started to scream. Lorraine followed the direction in which Lisa was looking, and saw the form that was frightening her friend. A shape distinctly resembling a monk wearing a black habit and hood stood only a short distance away from them.

The hood completely hid the face, so all they saw was a black void where the head should have been. They both said afterwards the figure seemed unusually wide – and it seemed to glow, making it vivid and clear in the darkness. Being probably less than a metre away, when Lorraine saw it she also screamed and closed her eyes instinctively, hoping the form would have disappeared when she opened them again. But when she did so the silent, motionless and somehow menacing figure was still there. It then began moving around as though looking for something. Meanwhile the boys, a little way ahead, turned to see what the girls were screaming about, for none of them could see anything.

Later Lisa told me the figure seemed to be about her height, five feet two inches (1.58 metres), but very wide. At first he seemed almost on top of her and she 'screamed uncontrollably and turned round in terror'. The boys were at a complete loss to know what was going on and Terry flashed his torch around but could detect nothing to account for the girls' obvious and sudden horror. Lisa added that the form seemed to 'glow black', the lower half of the hooded head seemed vaguely lighter, but no features were discernible.

By the time the girls had calmed down sufficiently to explain what they had seen, the wide, glowing monk-like form was no longer visible to either of them.

There is in existence a photograph taken in daylight in the area which shows a transparent monk-like figure which the photographer is totally unable to explain (sadly he will not permit me to reproduce the picture). Certainly it is the same area of the pathway where the girls saw the form that scared them. Is there a strange and frightening figure haunting the place that is visible to some people and not to others – perhaps women and not men, and perhaps sensitive to photography on occasions? Genuine paranormal activity often takes place when it is least expected, and touchings that have no physical explanation are by no means unknown. Silence accompanying apparitional forms seems to be the norm rather than the exception.

When David Crawford and his party reached Woody Bay, they were all in something of a state. The girls had obviously seen something that had shocked them greatly, and the boys realised this and so were unwilling for them to face going back to Martinhoe Manor by the same pathway.

It was eventually decided that the boys would return and fetch Terry's car. The thing was: which way to go – along the haunted pathway or a much longer way round? Armed only with the torch, they decided to brave the short way and follow the track they had used to reach Woody Bay. They set off in some trepidation and found themselves looking deep into the shadows bordering the track, but in the event they arrived back at the cabins without incident, much to their relief. They motored back to the bay, picked up the girls and brought them safely back, too.

Many times in the days that followed several of the friends would venture down the track in the evening and at night time in the hope of catching a glimpse or even taking a photograph of the ghost, if ghost it was. But to no avail. The girls vowed never to walk down that pathway at night ever again.

The path at Woody Bay, haunted by a molesting monk who 'glows black'

East of Mortehoe lies one of the most spectacular stretches of the north Devon coast path, apparently haunted by Sir Robert Chichester of Martinhoe

At the manor their story was accepted with serious interest. It seemed the chef had walked his dog along the path for some ten years and had never noticed anything untoward. On the other hand, since I first published this story some six years ago, I have received a number of reports from people, some local and some visitors to the area, who comment on curious experiences they say they have had on the the haunted pathway. In one instance a young couple were strolling down the path one evening when the girl suddenly screamed and pointed ahead. Her companion looked but saw nothing. She said she had seen the shadowy form of a fat man who seemed to emit a dim light all round him before he vanished, although there was no logical way he could have disappeared from view.

Mortehoe

The north Devon coast path here is truly spectacular and the stretch between Mortehoe and Ilfracombe is haunted.

Sir Robert Chichester of Martinhoe (according to Whitlock's *Folklore of Devon*, 1977) is thought to drive in his carriage up to the cliff face and through a narrow gap known as Sir Robert's Road.

A few years ago a correspondent informed me that he and his brother had been walking through Mortehoe one summer evening, thinking it was about time for a quiet pint rather than anything of a ghostly nature, when they turned a corner and found themselves face to face with a portly, red-faced gentleman dressed in the finery of years past.

He seemed much preoccupied and strode straight towards the brothers who parted to allow him to pass between them, which he did. As he did so, both brothers felt a cold draught, and were more than a little puzzled at his appearance and behaviour. They looked at each other and then behind them to see where the odd character had gone. Behind them the road was empty; there was no sign of the man and certainly nowhere he could have gone in the few seconds between him passing them and them looking round.

Next day they visited the public library at Ilfracombe and, mentioning their experience, they learned that the ghost of Sir Robert Chichester of Martinhoe was supposed to haunt the district. Although they 'haunted' Mortehoe and the coast path during the rest of their holiday, at night and during the day, they never encountered again anything resembling the mysterious and disappearing figure which had seemed so solid and normal in every way. Nor did they experience another icy draught of wind during that mild spell of weather.

North Tawton

I worked with Mitch Raper, the BBC producer and editor, on lots of radio programmes and he told me of the ghost he saw around North Tawton. He was with a friend, Paul.

Mitch and Paul were on vacation from Oxford at the time. Mitch then lived in Somerset, and Paul wanted to do a college production of an interesting little play the following term. They discovered that the playwright lived on a farm in Devon, and he had promised to put them both up for the night and explain all about the play.

The village was miles from the nearest railway station, but Mitch had a motorcycle. He and Paul set off and made good time until they were, according to their map, within a mile or so of the farm they were seeking. However, they were lost. They came across a T-junction with no signpost. And then Paul said suddenly: 'Let's ask him...', nodding in the direction he was looking. Following his gaze, Mitch saw a man wearing an old trilby hat and an ex-army cape. He was walking away from the lost travellers and, as he disappeared round a bend in the road, Mitch swung his bike round and they set off to ask for directions.

Round the corner, the road was clear as far ahead as they could see – nothing but flat moorland. Confused as to where the man could have gone so quickly, they steadily made their way along the deserted road, peering left and right to try to see him or discover his whereabouts. But they had no luck either way.

Then, abruptly, they were in a village. The only person visible was a woman pushing a pram and she explained where they should go: turn right at the bottom of the road. At first they thought it must have been her they saw earlier, but they decided they couldn't possibly have mistaken a woman pushing a pram for a man wearing a trilby and cape. Anyway, how could she have reached the village before them? They had been driving at about 20 miles an hour since seeing the mysterious man.

Arriving at last at their destination, they were regaled with coffee and a warm fire, and were beginning to enjoy themselves when they remembered the man. 'Something funny happened to us up on the road,' Mitch began. 'We saw a man and – ' Their host seemed delighted. 'You haven't seen the ghost, have you?' he asked, and called his wife from the kitchen. 'Mary, they've just seen the ghost!'

'It – just – vanished' Mitch said weakly.

'Oh, it always does that,' they were told. 'Usually at night.

Motorists get an awful shock. It suddenly appears in their head-lights and they have to brake and then there's no one there. They're furious when they realise what's happened.'

'We had an argument about which way it was going,' Paul added.

'I know – other people say the same thing... I was telling them it's unusual to see it in daylight,' the author commented, turning to his wife.

Next morning dawned bright and clear, and after leaving the farm Mitch and Paul retraced their steps from the evening before. There was no wall, tree, hedge or anywhere someone could have hidden.

Looking back, Mitch said two things always struck him as odd about the incident. It was definitely not frightening or even scary, and then there was what seemed very much like proof which arrived ten years later.

All that time after the event Mitch was having a meal with an antique dealer and his wife, and the conversation turned to the supernatural. The wife was most interested in Mitch's story and she seemed to know a lot about ghosts. 'Did the figure have feet that touched the ground?' she asked. And she had hit the nail on the head, for Mitch and Paul had argued about whether the figure was approaching or going away from them.

They had also argued about how it had walked – not plodding slowly or walking quickly, but with feet that almost 'twinkled' (Mitch couldn't think of a better word) just clear of the grass. 'No,' Mitch told his friend, 'It wasn't touching the ground. The feet just seemed to go to and fro.' 'Then it was a ghost,' Mitch was told.

Years later, as guest speaker at a hotel in Somerset, I related this experience and was surprised when a couple looked at each other in astonishment and told me they had had an almost identical experi-ence. As far as I could judge, it occurred in the same area. The male figure they saw was dressed oddly: it wore a trilby hat and a cape. It was daylight, late afternoon, and the couple never could decide whether it was coming or going. It also disappeared in mysterious circumstances – so mysterious, in fact, that they returned a few days later and went over the whole area again, but they never did discover a solution to the mystery. I may say that in my talk I had not revealed the exact location, only saying it was in a quiet part of Devon. The couple related their so similar experience and said where they had seen the curious figure. They were astonished when I revealed that Mitch and Paul had come across the same thing at the same place twenty years earlier.

Okehampton

A very ancient and restless ghost (said to be that of wealthy merchant Benjamin Gayer, four times mayor of Okehampton) reputedly haunts the area and troubled the townsfolk here as long ago as 1884 when *The Western Antiquary* carried an account of the measures taken to exorcise the unwelcome inhabitant.

One archdeacon and twenty-three clergymen took part in the exorcism. For some reason they invoked the entity in various classical languages but – perhaps not surprisingly – without any success. At length, addressed in Arabic, a reply was reportedly obtained: 'Now thou art come, I must be gone'. The phantom was then apparently compelled to take the form of a colt which was ridden to Cranmere Pool on Dartmoor. It was released and given the time-honoured task approbated by exorcists of making trusses of sand and binding them into ropes – an impossible feat. There, according to tradition, the matter rests to this day.

The ruined Norman castle is haunted by a ghostly black dog whose glance is said to mean death within a year to the beholder. Another ghostly sight that may have been seen here is the skeletal coach carrying the wicked Lady Howard which is driven by a headless coachman and is supposed to pass the castle on its way to her Ladyship's home at Fitzford near Tavistock. She was by all accounts a formidable woman who may have murdered all four of her husbands. A former deputy keeper at the castle told me he once saw a figure he took to be the famous phantom Lady Howard sitting on a stone, combing her hair. As he approached, she vanished.

Opposite: Okehampton Castle

The White Hart Hotel at Okehampton may look like an early nineteenth century coaching inn, but the interior is much older, and is haunted by a playful child

The spectre has long been reputed to haunt the castle grounds and a path nearby is named Lady Howard's Walk, but whether this is an historical reference or the result of the ghost walking is difficult to substantiate.

Other Okehampton hauntings include the White Hart Hotel in the town centre where there is, reportedly, the ghost of a boy called Peter who delights in playing hide-and-seek with real children and who is blamed for tinkering with toys at the hotel. It is said that Peter's mother was murdered here and he is searching for her – usually upstairs in the oldest part of the building. In 1996 a Ghost Club Society member, unaware of any reputed haunting, encountered a boy who vanished inexplicably, and then learned that she and her husband had probably seen the harmless hotel ghost.

Parkham

Here, at a house called Boscombe, according to researcher and historian J RW Coxhead, 'a queer legend was once attached'.

The parish of Parkham lies south of the road that runs out of Bideford round Barnstaple Bay and towards Cornwall. The road is now familiar to visitors as the A39, but few venture off it to visit the many delightful villages, each with a story all their own.

Long ago, it is said, the lady of Boscombe died and in due course her body was buried in the village churchyard. When the mourners returned to the house after the funeral they were astonished to see the deceased lady seated in her accustomed chair at the head of the table – or rather the recognisable apparition of the lady.

Thereafter the house was haunted by the spectre of the lady – why, nobody seems to know. It became such a nuisance, surprising and sometimes frightening by its unexpected appearance to relatives, friends and visitors, that eventually the family asked the parish priest to rid the house of the ghost. This the priest agreed to do and having, he believed, successfully performed the full service of exorcism, he went on to banish the spectre to the sea shore until it could bind sand 'to make bands of the same'. So, we are told, the spectre was condemned to remain on the sea shore for ever since the task was an impossible one. Why then, asks the intrepid ghost hunter, are there no reports of any such figure being seen thereabouts?

Sampford Peverell

This small place east of Tiverton has become famous in psychical circles because of activities that have become known as 'The Sampford Ghost'. There was considerable notoriety here around two centuries ago when the local rector, Caleb Colton, published the story, including his own experiences, in *The Narrative of the Sampford Ghost* in 1810.

The village home of John Chave was reportedly affected by a wealth of typical poltergeist phenomena: loud and unexplained noises, movement of objects, raps and knockings, footsteps, and the women of the house beaten black and blue by invisible hands!

As with many poltergeist infestations, the whole affair ended unsatisfactorily with suggestions that John Chave was faking the disturbances to obtain a cheap purchase of the property. But in fact he never bought the house and, although the Rev. Caleb Colton (who was criticised for his part in the affair) offered £250 – a lot of money in those days – to anyone who could solve the mystery, the money was never claimed.

There were other outside witnesses, including the governor of the county gaol who claimed to see spectacular happenings, but years later it was discovered the house had double walls and a passage between. Then there were whispers that John Chave may have been in league with smugglers and that he spread the story of ghosts to keep people away from the house. The Sampford Ghost seems to be a matter of 'you pays your money and you takes your choice'.

Shebbear

A few miles north-east of Holsworthy this village has a haunted stone, or so the story goes. Situated just outside the churchyard, it is known as the Devil's Stone, because it has long been regarded as a hiding place for the Devil himself. It is said that he will continue to hide there and plague the village if the stone is not turned once each year – on the fifth of November.

The whole story seems to be the result of Christianising a pagan custom whereby each year the bell ringers make as much noise as possible to frighten the Devil away from the Stone. They then leave the church, among shouts of encouragement from the assembled audience, and turn the ancient Devil's Stone – which is actually a large lump of conglomerate, something that is not found anywhere in the immediate vicinity.

It might be interesting to see exactly what *would* happen if the Stone was not turned one year, but the powers that be were horrified when I suggested such a course of action! Such is the hold of pagan customs.

The village public house, The Devil's Stone Inn, is supposed to

Opposite: The Devil's Stone at Shebbear

be haunted by the ghost of a little girl aged about seven years who is seen accompanied by a man with a grey beard. The story is that the man was murdered at the inn and the little girl, his daughter, was with him at the time. So perhaps this is a case of two individual ghosts, one that of a dead person – a man who was murdered – and one of a person living at the time of the murder...

Spreyton

In the 1950s and '60s, according to ghost hunter Andrew Green, Fuidge Manor, then a hotel, at Spreyton east of Okehampton was haunted by the ghost of a diminutive monk.

One visitor, Mrs Forshaw, stated that she had encountered 'a small figure dressed in a monk's habit' at the top of a stairway at about 5 o'clock one late afternoon.

Green reported that 'some seemed to think it was a young novice, others that it was a dwarf ordained into the Brotherhood', but why he or she should haunt the establishment does not seem to have been ascertained.

A later visitor to the hotel, who was unaware of such stories, related almost tripping over 'something' at the top of the stairs one evening. At first she thought it was a dog, but when 'it' scuttled off along the corridor away from her she realised it was a human being, perhaps a child. It made no sound and seemed to be wearing a long brown smock or something of the sort. As she followed, apologising for the surprise of her presence, she discovered that whatever had been there had completely disappeared. There had been no doors opened and closed, and nothing had passed her...

In 1996 I was in the area making enquiries about local legends when I was introduced to an elderly resident who does not wish to be identified. He told me – before I had said anything – that of course the place was haunted by the unhappy 'dwarfs' who were once housed nearby in a community. He explained that in his youth (this would be before the First World War) he knew people who claimed they had seen small figures in the village, figures that always seemed to be dressed in long habit-like cloaks. One or two occupants of houses also said they sometimes glimpsed similar figures, usually near the staircase.

I did try to discover more about this community, but I did not succeed in finding any more information in the short time I was there. If you see the ghost of a small figure in Spreyton, do please let me know.

Stowford

Hayne Manor House has long been reputed to be haunted by the ghost of a pageboy, murdered, so people say, by the butler and his wife. However, details are scarce to come by.

There are three large stones to the west of the village and each is commonly reported to mark a haunted location. One marks the spot where the body of the pageboy was buried beneath the branches of a beech tree. A second indicates where a huntsman managed to get eaten by his own hounds – and the awful sounds of the barbaric and monstrous meal are still reputed to be heard from time to time. And the third stone marks the grave of John Cator whose fate is not recorded, but whose ghost, it seems, still walks.

Hayne Manor House is also credited with a spectral black dog, especially common in this part of the West Country, while a headless man haunts the terrace. Not surprisingly, he has never been identified, but neither has the little old lady who occasionally walks silently and harmlessly through the King Charles Room.

Tetcott

The area around this village, south of Holsworthy, has long been said to be haunted, especially in the vicinity of what remains of the Queen Anne mansion. It was once the ancestral home of the Arscotts, the last of whom died in 1788.

A keen and formidable hunter in his lifetime, this last of the line was a strong and individual personality (as many ghosts were in their earthly life), and is thought to have appeared on many occasions since his death, usually mounted on his favourite horse and accompanied by his famous pack of hunting dogs.

He was indisputably a great huntsman, and there is an 18th-century ballad devoted to Arscott the Huntsman which contains these lines:

> When the full moon is shining clear as day,
> John Arscott still hunteth the country, they say,
> You may see him on Blackbird, and hear in full cry
> The pack from Pencarrow to Dazzard go by.

Antony Coxe told me that this John Arscott had distinctly odd behaviour: he kept a pet toad which answered to his call and took food with him at the table. He was also in the habit of taking a bottle of flies to church to feed the spiders, and he was known to throw apples at the parson when his sermon was not to his liking.

The arresting spectacle of Arscott on his horse and surrounded by his dogs would seem to be a collective atmospheric photograph type of apparition, something that reappears by a quirk of nature where the original once was. Interestingly, this type of ghostly activity also runs down and ultimately ceases entirely, but it does so gradually: the visual aspect at first becomes transparent and invisible, leaving the sounds that accompanied the phenomenon. In due course the sounds fade too, and then nothing remains of the long-lasting spectre. However, some people may become aware of an atmosphere and may sense 'something' in the area where the manifestation used to be seen. Horses and dogs in particular may show signs of fright at haunted localities, apparently seeing or sensing something invisible to their human companions.

At Tetcott and round about, sightings of the mounted huntsman and his hounds are few and far between these days, but there are occasional reports of the sounds of a galloping horse and a pack of dogs emanating from nowhere, passing the witnesses and disappearing into the distance. It is now well over 200 years since the original John Arscott left the land of the living and so it is to be expected that the last vestige of this interesting psychic phenomenon will soon disappear for ever.

Tiverton

Author Arthur Farquharson-Coe once told me about a highly unusual ghost that haunts or haunted the drive and lodge of a large estate near Tiverton.

A phantom car and phantom driver, no less, have been heard to pass up the drive and stop at the door of Worth Lodge. It sounds like a powerful modern engine, according to witnesses, the noise accelerating up the drive before dying away. At the lodge itself, sounds have been heard of a car door opening and then closing, followed by the creak of a gate and then silence.

No one ever sees the car, the driver or whoever gets out of the car. But many people have corroborated the story of the sounds which apparently happen at various times on various days throughout the year. And there have been curious happenings reported at the house.

A family who moved into Worth Lodge reported hearing the phantom car soon after they took possession in 1970. Although they never saw it or anyone associated with it, the wife did once encounter the ghost of a young man inside the lodge. He seemed to be trying to impart some information before he disappeared, but whether it was anything to do with the mysterious invisible car and its equally curious and invisible passengers we have yet to learn.

Tiverton Castle has a sad ghost, the phantom of a lady who had been married only a few hours before she died. The story goes that a large wooden box, long a part of the castle furniture, was used in a game of hide and seek organised by the younger guests at a wedding party. While the older guests looked on in amused tolerance, the youngsters followed the bride and her husband as they entered into the light-hearted game.

Soon the game spread to other parts of the castle and the bride saw the large box which she decided would make an ideal hiding place. Carefully folding her voluminous wedding gown about her, she climbed inside and lowered the heavy lid.

Within minutes the sounds of laughter and excited shouts told her the seekers were coming. In her excitement at the prospect of being discovered, she let the lid close completely – and heard an ominous click as a spring lock snapped into place. She did not know it, but this meant the lid could be opened only from outside.

As time passed the bride attempted to lift the lid and found to her horror that she could not shift it. She cried out, but the faint sounds were drowned by the happy wedding guests. She tried again and again to push open the lid, but it would not shift in the slightest.

Hours later when the game was long over and all the guests had searched the castle calling her name and urging herself to reveal herself as the winner, someone pointed to the overlooked chest – but it appeared to be locked. Eventually the lid was removed and the dead bride uncovered. Since then, the ghost of a woman in a long white dress has reportedly been seen running through the rooms of the castle, a figure that soon disappears and cannot be found anywhere – until the next time.

Such a story is told of a number of castles and country houses, especially Bramshill and Marwell Hall, both in Hampshire, and I have spoken to people who believe they have caught a glimpse of the ghost bride in both houses. At Bramshill there is an enormous carved chest in the entrance hall, proudly labelled 'The Bride's Chest'.

Opposite: Tiverton Castle

Tiverton (Chettiscombe)

A strange story of ghosts and treasure comes from Chettiscombe, just north of Tiverton. Martin Dunsford in his *Historical Memoirs of Tiverton*, published in 1790, reported a tradition that a considerable quantity of treasure had been concealed near the ruined chapel of St Mary. In spite of many attempts over the years to recover it, nothing was found. Then, in the sixteenth century, two farmers made a determined effort to locate the treasure.

About 9 o'clock one evening, the treasure seekers approached the hallowed walls where they were startled almost out of their wits by the sudden appearance of an enormous white owl that flew silently from a broken window, settled in front of them and appeared to address them! The two men had the impression the bird – or whatever it was – imparted to them the information that considerable treasure lay hidden in a certain part of the adjoining farmyard and that if they would carefully dig there and diligently attend the labourers, to prevent purloining, they would undoubtedly find it.

The seekers took careful note of what they had learned, quickly employed the necessary workmen and, keeping a close eye on everyone involved, succeeded in uncovering, according to the legend, 'a valuable deposit of treasure'.

It cannot but be interesting to find that even today there are stories of a huge white owl 'haunting' the site of St Mary's Chapel, as it has, it would seem, for centuries.

Tiverton (Huntsham Barton)

Among the records of the Paraphysical Laboratory is a report of curious happenings in a three-storey Regency period farmhouse at Huntsham Barton, which is six miles north of Tiverton.

One March, Anthony Cross and his wife Janet moved into the house and a few days later Anthony was aware of an unmistakable 'presence' in the house. As he became aware of it, so he found himself completely immobilised and unable to move hand or foot or even speak for about a minute. Before he mentioned the episode to his wife, she said she had to talk to him about something odd that had happened: she had had an almost identical experience.

Late that night Janet heard footsteps outside the bedroom door. She thought it must be her son and went back to sleep (she subsequently found it had not been her son at all). She awoke two hours later to find herself completely immobilised. Anthony awoke at the same time and also could not move. Both husband and wife watched each other trying to speak and not being able to.

After an exorcism was carried out at the house, objects, especially photographs, were moved in circumstances that precluded human responsibility. After the blessing, both the husband and wife felt things were better, but they were reluctant to sleep in the same room. When they moved to another part of the house, the feelings of immobilisation occurred yet again.

There is no rational explanation, but perhaps this was more of a physiological problem than a psychical one, although the experienced Paraphysical Society treated it as an outburst of spontaneous psychic phenomena. If that is what it was, it would appear to have been a unique manifestation.

Tiverton (Knightshayes Court)

One summer day in 1997 Susan Penn and her family walked into a mystery at Knightshayes Court, the striking Victorian gothic mansion just off the A396 Tiverton to Bampton road.

A rare survival of the work of William Burges, the flamboyant 19th-century architect, this remarkable house is a rich mixture of medieval romanticism and lavish decoration. For many years it was the home of the Heathcoat-Amory family and on the death of the second Sir John Heathcoat-Amory in 1972 it was bequeathed to The National Trust. In August 1998 the assistant to the Property Manager at Knightshayes told me that, as far as she is aware, they have no ghosts and the Victorian family home has a very friendly atmosphere.

However, I have in my possession a report from Susan Penn and her husband and two teenage children (all of whom do not usually see ghosts) who plainly saw a seemingly solid and normal figure on the teak staircase during a visit. They had been the first visitors to the house that day and they originally thought it must have been one of the resident family or a National Trust official. They described the figure to me as a tubby man in old-fashioned clothes with mutton-chop whiskers and wearing glasses. He stood close to the wall and seemed to be interested in the people visiting the house.

As my informant and her family began to go up the stairs, apparently watched by the stationary person, they were astonished to find that the solid-looking and relaxed figure had completely disappeared. One second earlier they had all independently seen the man and there was nowhere anyone could possibly have gone in that very short time: the time it takes to lift a foot to mount a stair. They spent the rest of their visit puzzling over the mystery and keeping an eye open for the tubby gentleman, but they never came across anyone remotely resembling the figure they had clearly seen on the stairs.

Later, reading the house guide-book, they found the picture of William Burges (1827-81) who had built the beautiful staircase, just about all he had built of the interior of the house. They all immediately stated that was the man they had encountered.

Later still, in the garden, the two teenagers came running back to their parents saying they had heard the roar of an aeroplane flying very low but they could not detect anything to account for the noise. The sound ended with an awful crashing bang and then silence. Both the girl and her brother agreed about the noises they had heard and it was only when they were all back home and reading through the guide-book that they learned about the tragedy which happened towards the end of the Second World War. Knightshayes had been used as a hospital during the First World War and as a Rest Home for American servicemen during the Second. Joyce, Lady Heathcoat-Amory, takes up the story in her 'Introduction' to the *Official Guide to Knightshayes Court*:

Opposite: The gatehouse of Weare Giffard Hall, near Great Torrington, where a churlish ghost tells visitors to 'Get thee gone'

'Very near the end of the war a sad tragedy took place. It was the custom for departed occupants to return from their airfields in order to "buzz" the house, which meant flying up the park almost at tree level, to applause and clapping from the terrace. One fighter pilot, alas, lost his life, his plane hitting the tops of several trees. The clearing away of the broken trees after the war was, more happily, the beginning of the Garden in the Wood.'

Weare Giffard

The gatehouse of mellow Weare Giffard Hall is said to be the start of the walk taken by the ghostly Sir Walter Giffard who died in 1243. His walk ends at the nearby church, if ends is the right word, for if we accept enduring personal experiences the ghost has walked this route for over 750 years and he is still walking.

The story goes that Sir Walter is seeking his wife, but I can't help wondering why he searches so earnestly for so long and why in the area of the church. The truth of the whole matter is lost in the mists of time and now only the ghost remains for those with eyes to see it – the last vestige of some long forgotten event echoing down the centuries. When I was there some years ago a record of the ghost and its appearances was preserved inside the church.

There have been reports here too of a ghostly crusader, and there is also said to be the ghost of a lout: perhaps the most loutish phantom on record! Every single witness who has met with the ghost of what appears to be a common man of five centuries ago has heard, much to their surprise, the roughly spoken words: 'Get thee gone...'

The origin of this ghost and his seemingly churlish behaviour is not known either, but for those who have heard them the words echo strangely in the mind afterwards: 'Get thee gone... Get thee gone...'

West Worlington

This village, some nine miles south of South Molton, is said to hide buried treasure amid the scanty remains of the fortified manor house of Affeton.

As long ago as 1858, writer J D'Israeli discovered that the 'secret' practices of Sir 'Judas' Stukeley at the time of James I throw light on the local tradition of treasure and a guardian spirit in the area. Affeton was once the residence of 'this wretched man'.

Country people hereabouts, stated D'Israeli, 'have long entertained the notion that a hidden treasure lies at the bottom of a well in the grounds, guarded by some supernatural power'.

This Sir 'Judas' Stukeley was in fact Sir Lewis Stukeley, Vice-Admiral of Devon, the man who arrested Sir Walter Raleigh in 1618, on the orders of James I, and the man who is reputed to have made false statements about the celebrated Devonian to blacken his character.

There is some evidence and considerable supposition that Stukeley was adequately, some say extravagantly, rewarded for his treachery and there is also more than a little evidence that he clipped pieces off gold coins that passed through his hands.

Be that as it may, none of this reputed treasure ever seems to have been located and from time immemorial there have been reports of odd happenings and strange misfortune affecting anyone seriously attempting to find it.

As recently as 1995 three men – a father and his two sons – took metal detectors to the vicinity and were working the likely area when the father suffered a heart attack and neither of his sons could get the car started.

With the help of a local inhabitant, they did get their father to hospital where he eventually recovered, but none of them ever returned to seek the treasure.

To this day they are certain there is something not of this world protecting it. One of the sons left his metal detector at the site, but he never bothered to return to collect it: 'Whatever is there is welcome to it...' he told me.

Winkleigh

If frustration, unhappiness, remorse, loneliness, traumatic happenings, introverted lives and violent death can result in ghosts and hauntings, then West Chapple Farm near Winkleigh should be seriously haunted. And it is! It saw an abundance of such harrowing events that resulted in no less than three violent deaths. And Winkleigh, so much at the centre of the whole affair, would still appear to harbour echoes of that awful time.

In September 1975 the farm had divided ownership which made it, as one investigator put it, 'an emotional penitentiary in which each was the jailer, each jailed.' For years it had been a weird place, a place where people could hide or behave in an abnormal fashion without discovery. Its very peculiar locality amid hidden valleys and high hedges fostered and fed secretiveness and an unhealthy atmosphere that resulted in tragedy – and ghosts.

The Luxton family were well-known in the area for centuries, and they always took an interest in the community and in the village. Robert Luxton (1872-1939), the father of the last three members of the family, knew all about the ghostly coach that had been seen in Winkleigh. He opposed the building of the community hall in the centre of the village, mumbling something about a curse and secrets that lay in an underground passageway that must never be revealed...

From the death of their father in 1939, 'the farm where time stood still' was run by the two brothers, Robbie and Alan, together with their sister, Frances. Like their father, they had been born at West Chapple Farm and had lived there all their lives. None of them ever married: 'nobody was good enough for them', the locals used to say. Alan had been engaged at one time, but it all ended in tears.

He had wanted to sell his share of the farm and move on, but his brother and sister would not agree. There were tremendous rows and the three continued to live in disharmony until eventually there was such an explosion of animosity, unhappiness and frustration that they all met their deaths. Alan's body was found with his arms folded, but the top of his head blown away. Frances died on her hands and knees, and Robbie lay nearby, with heavy cuts to his face and having died from massive head injuries.

Opposite: Winkleigh, where the secretive and sheltered streets are apparently still haunted by the ghosts of three members of one family

76

There had long been stories of ghosts and hauntings at the farm. Less phantom forms, perhaps, than overwhelming atmospheric disturbances. One person who visited soon after the deaths sensed 'an atmosphere of bitterness and despair... an overpowering evil stench.' Another, who knew the Luxtons, found the place 'distinctly creepy'.

When I was there in 1987 I talked with a number of people who were convinced, from personal experience, that the place was haunted; 'had been for ages,' one said, 'and always will be'.

Winkleigh, too, has its ghosts. My wife and I met people who believed they had seen ghosts of members of the West Chapple Farm Luxton family in Winkleigh – after the end of the line had come with the violent deaths of Frances, Robert and Alan. The narrow streets still seem to guard the memory of this strange family and maybe some of them do still visit the quiet places they knew and where some of them are buried.

Certainly there are people living in Winkleigh today who have encountered the silent and frightening forms of the three dead Luxtons in the secretive and sheltered streets of a village haunted by its past.

Woolacombe

Woolacombe Sands, part of magnificent Morte Bay, west of Ilfracombe, where my wife and I have enjoyed some wonderful walks, is reputed to be haunted by one of the murderers of Thomas à Becket. I have met three people who, independently, believe they have seen the unmistakable form of an aristocratic man in 12th-century attire, in each case in the distance in bright and sunny weather.

Interestingly, I once spent a night at haunted Slaybrook, a wonderful old house in Kent that had been a hostelry in the 12th century. It stands less than a mile from Saltwood Castle where Becket's murder was plotted. The story goes that the knights involved in

Opposite: On a fine day on Woolacombe Sands it is hard to imagine that it might be haunted – but it is on just such days that the ghost appears

the murder did not return to Saltwood after the deed was done, but spent the night at the nearby hostelry (where echoes of their presence have remained ever since) before leaving the district the next day.

One of those knights was William de Tracy and he fled to Devon, hoping to lie low for a while and remain undetected. But, according to Lady Rosalind of Northcote, he was cursed after his death to wander at night over Woolacombe Sands (and some say at nearby Braunton Burrows) for all eternity.

Be that as it may, it is not too difficult to find local people who not only accept this story and its aftermath, but who actually claim to have seen for themselves the spectral form of Sir William de Tracy among the stillness and beauty of Woolacombe Sands.

Acknowledgements

The author acknowledges with gratitude the help and co-operation he has received from everyone concerned in the research and writing of this book, and would especially like to mention: the late Herbert Benson and The Paraphysical Library, David Crawford, Joan Dimond, Arthur Farquharson-Coe, the late Daniel Farson, The Ghost Club Society, Valerie H Goold, Robin and Sue Gray, Marion Harris, the late JW Herries, the late Antony Hippisley Coxe, The National Trust, Barnstaple, Honiton and Ilfracombe Tourist Information Centres and all the other information bureaux who have helped; the late Air Commodore Carter Jonas, Rosemary Leach, Rodney Legg, Roy Harley Lewis, Bob Mann, the late Rosemary Parker, Mitch Raper of the BBC, Maxine Todd, the late James Turner, Harold Unsworth, Jane White of Bossiney Books, Michael Williams, Tim Wormleighton, Senior Archivist at Devon County Council, and last, but by no means least, the author acknowledges once again the support, help and advice he has received from his wife Joyce.